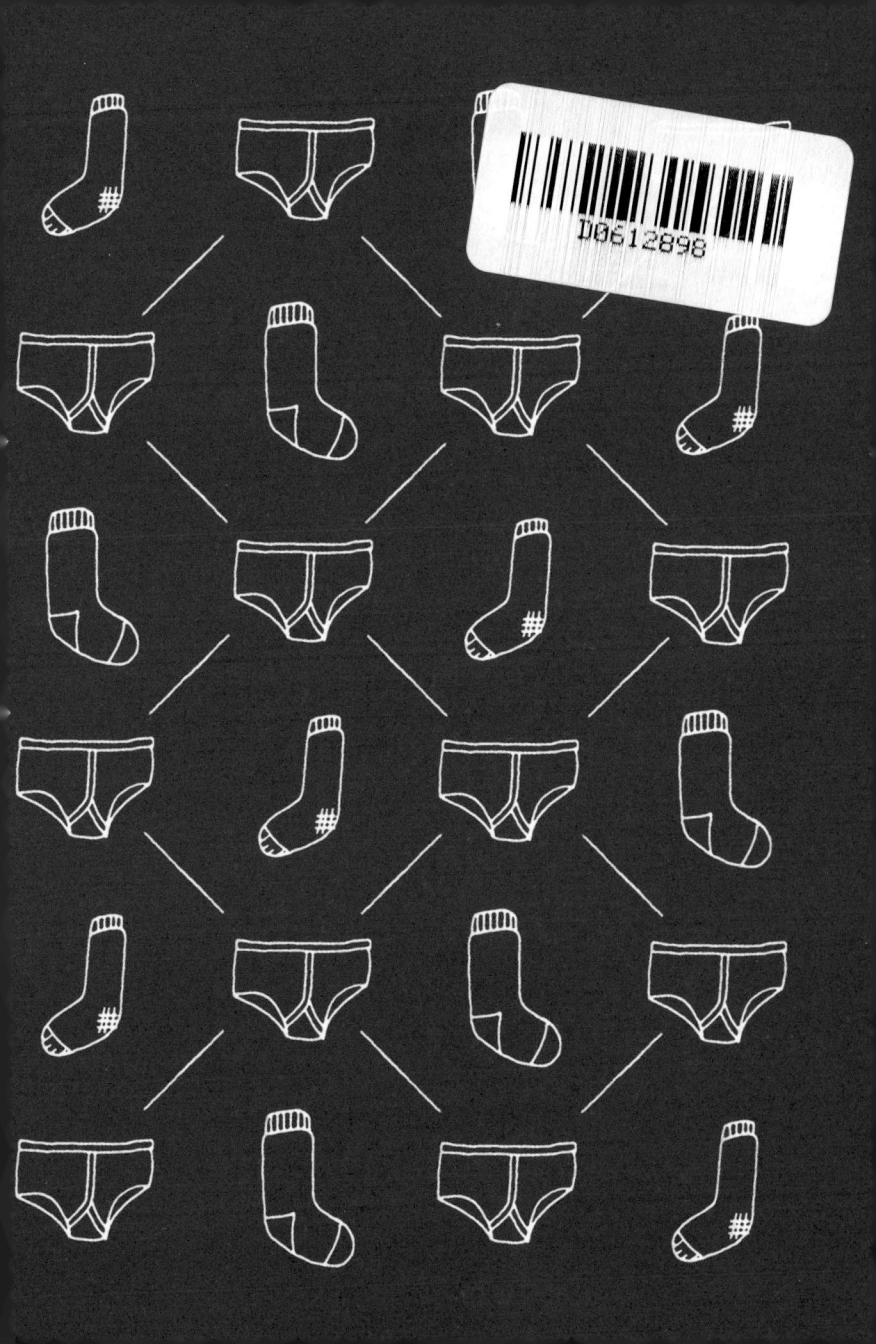

D0612898

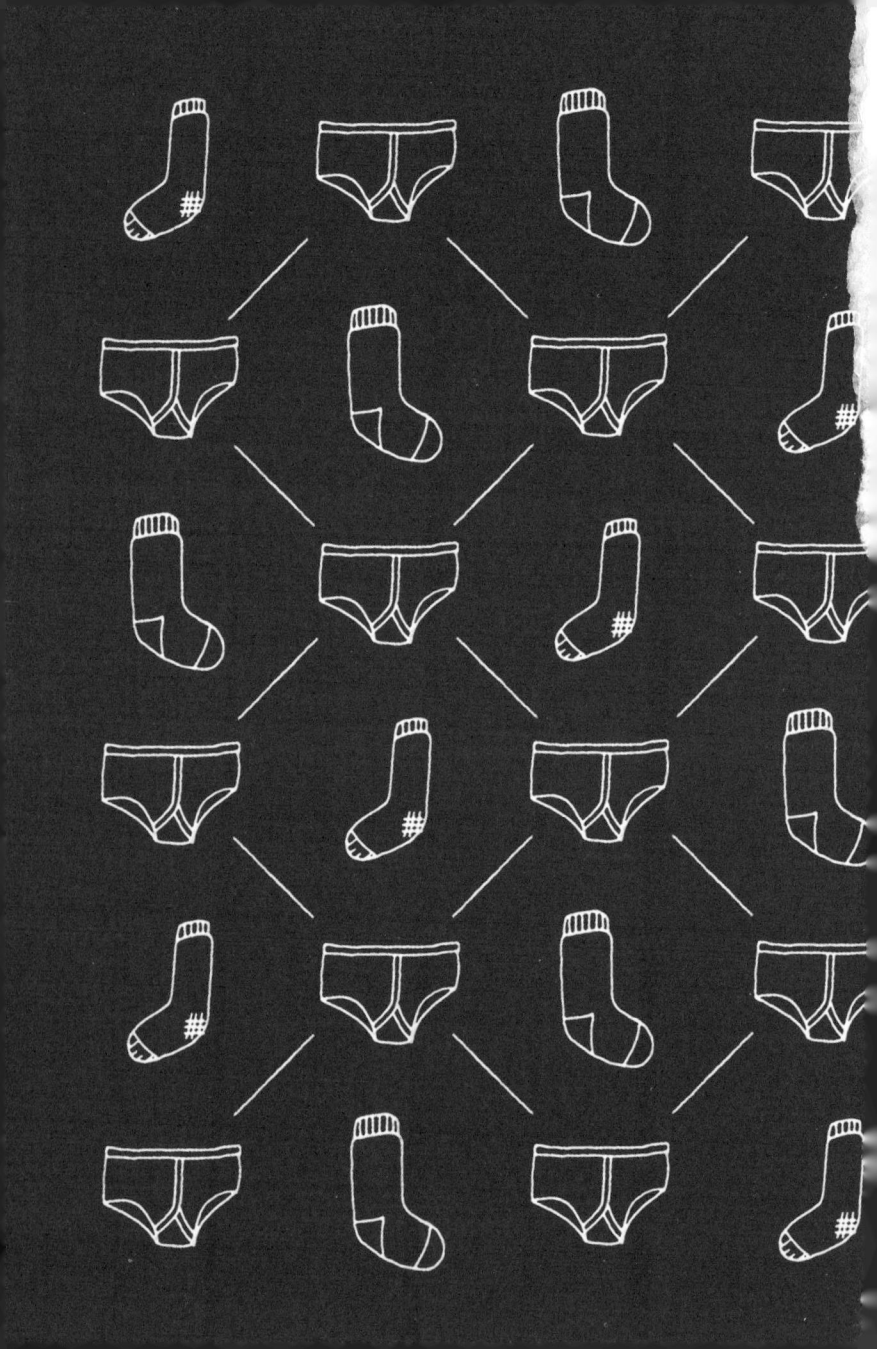

WHY BOYS NEED PARENTS

Alex Beckerman

CHRONICLE BOOKS
SAN FRANCISCO

Text copyright © 2015 by
Chronicle Books LLC.

All rights reserved. No part of
this book may be reproduced
in any form without written
permission from the publisher.

Library of Congress Cataloging-in-
Publication Data available.

ISBN: 978-1-4521-4734-5

Manufactured in China

Designed by Ben Kither
Picture Editor, Julien Tomasello

Chronicle Books LLC
680 Second Street,
San Francisco, California, 94107
www.chronicklebooks.com

10 9 8 7 6 5 4

Dedicated to boys everywhere, young and old.

Introduction.

The invention of fire occurred when Ogg Jr. decided to see what happens when you rub rocks together near the sulfur pit. Fire was born.

This led immediately to the invention of the time-out.

Boys will be boys. Unfortunately, they will also be arsonists, wrecking balls, flooders, and eight-limbed ninjas of destruction. It is their nature. Boys are driven to explore, whether it's the mysteries of life or the contents of their own nose. The same impulse that inspires them to experiment and discover also tells them to cut their own hair. It is what has brought us electricity, space exploration, and the vaccine for polio.

It's also what brought us Chernobyl, telemarketing, and the Great Bathroom Flood of 2013.

We want to nurture their exuberant drive, but we also want the species to continue. This is where you come in. If you have a son, you perform heroics every day. You dam geysers, extinguish explosions, patch holes, and bandage boo-boos. You've been mooned and karate-chopped. You have had a child pee in your shoes *while you were wearing them.* You've survived juice stains, waterlogged phones, dropped laptops, and multiple ER visits, and miraculously, the boys have too.

Boys need parents. But the secret truth is that parents need boys. It would be awfully boring without them, wouldn't it?

Still, it might be nice to go one full week without having to call a plumber.

Perhaps he'll be one when he grows up. In the meantime, keep going, have fun, and hope that the grandkids are girls.

To teach him the importance of utensils.

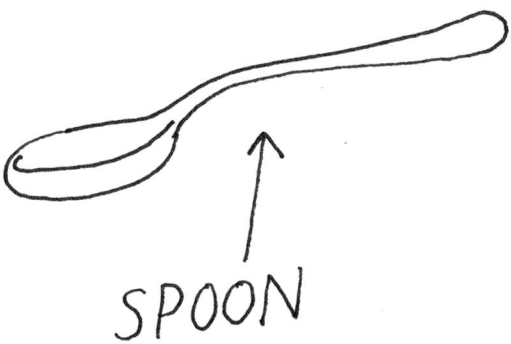

NOT A SPOON

WE ARE ROBOTS

Because not everything needs to be a costume.

Because chocolate syrup is not a food group.

Because "snips, snails, and puppy dog tails" isn't supposed to be taken literally.

SIGH...

Because every superhero
needs a sidekick.

So it won't freeze that way.

NASA

Because Grandma can still change her will.

Because that's not what you meant by "Clean it inside and out."

Dad will love this!

To help them rethink their priorities.

WAY AHEAD
OF SCHEDULE

DUDE,
WHAT'S YOUR PROBLEM

Because someday, he'll be allowed to drive.

THE ERRATIC LINE WORK EXPRESSES THE ARTIST'S FRAME OF MIND.
AND THE COLOR IS A METAPHOR FOR WHAT HE JUST DID TO HIS DIAPER. EXTRAORDINARY TALENT.

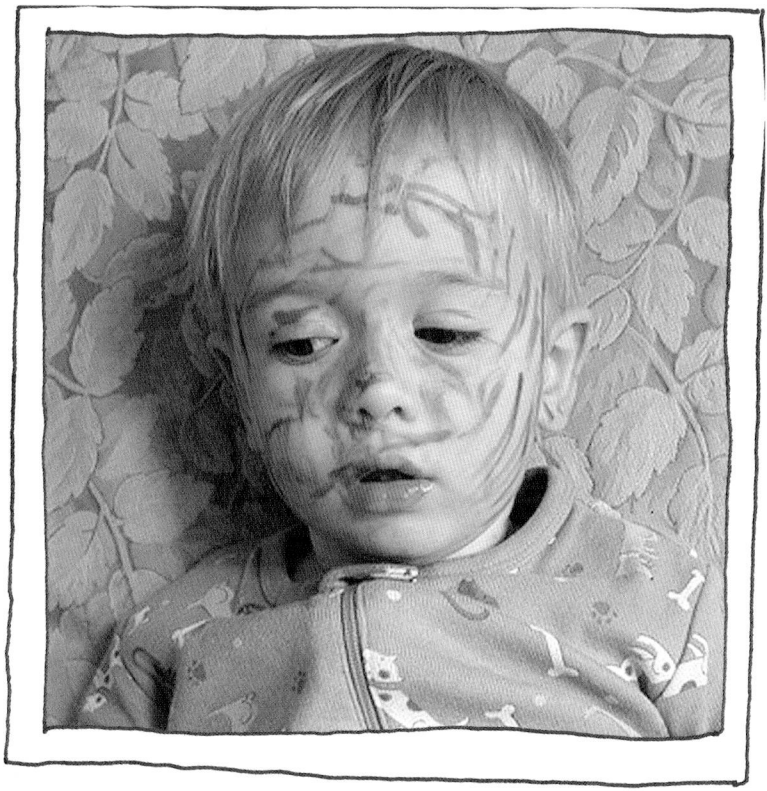

To explain that a self-portrait is not a portrait done on one's self.

What cake?

To keep them honest.

Because we aren't there yet.

To sing back-up.

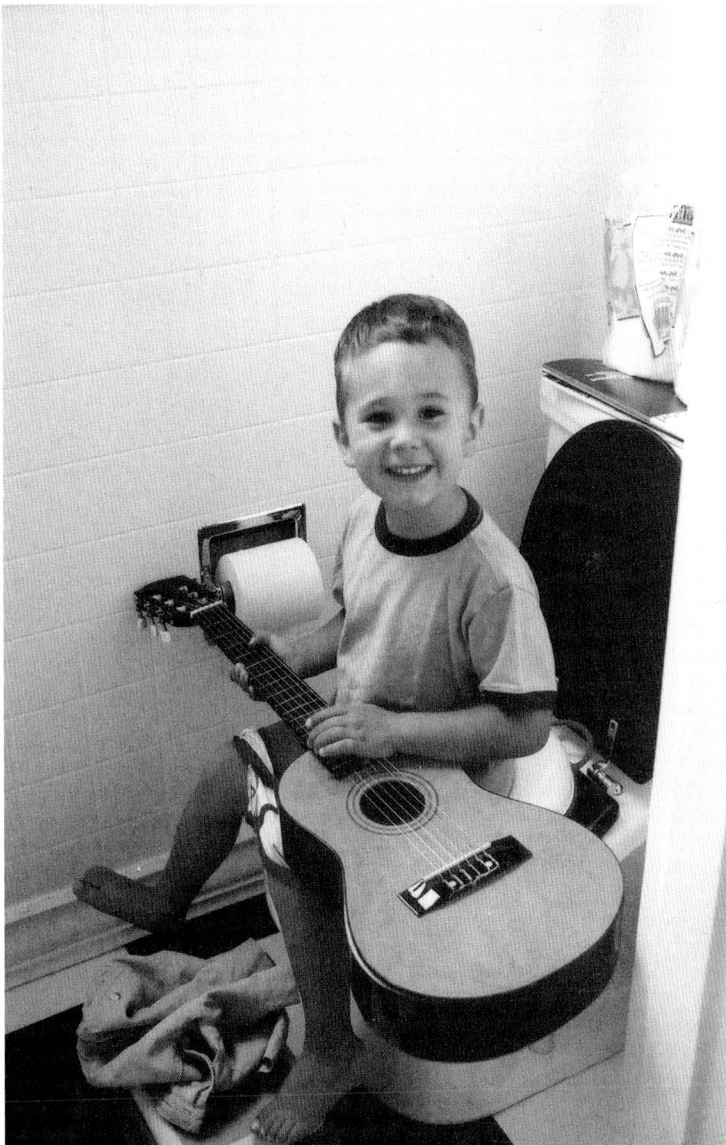

Because the Creature from the Black Lagoon is not touching the white door with those hands.

Because you can't be leader of the pack with chocolate sundae on your face.

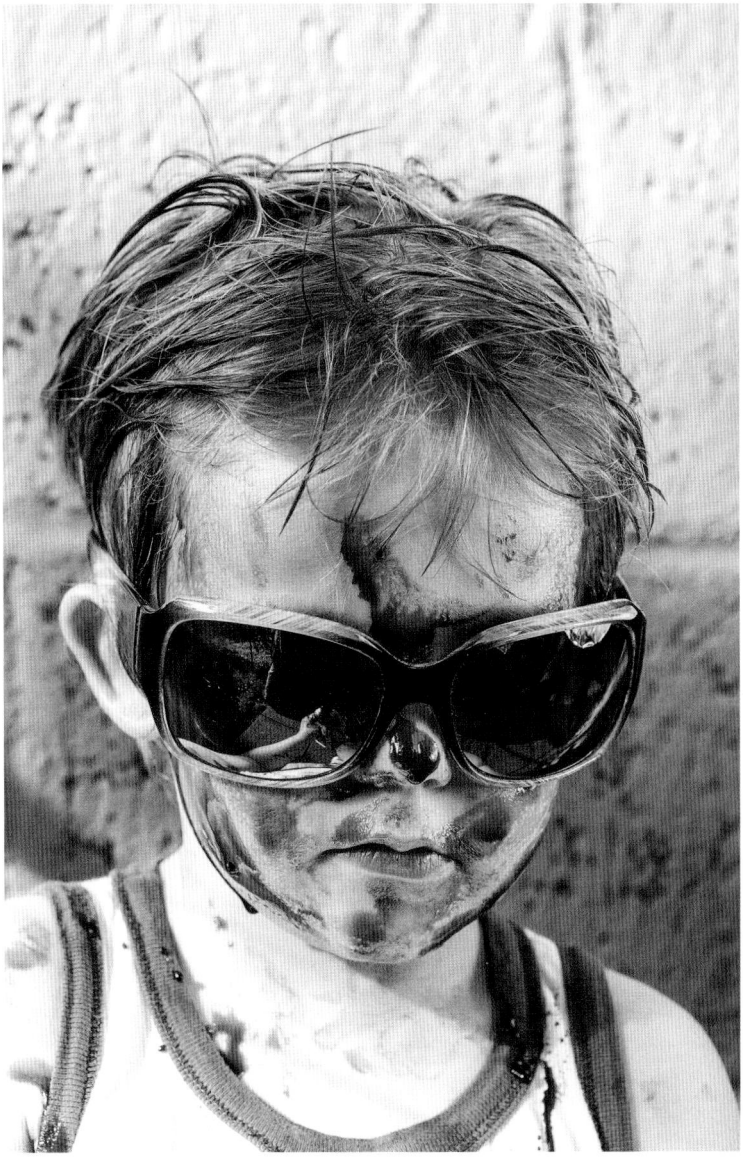

To referee their cage-match pillow fights.

hello.

To check for pool sharks.

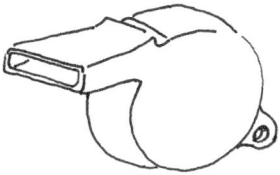

To give them a running start.

This is the good life Mr. Kitty.

Because if it weren't for you, he wouldn't even be wearing underpants.

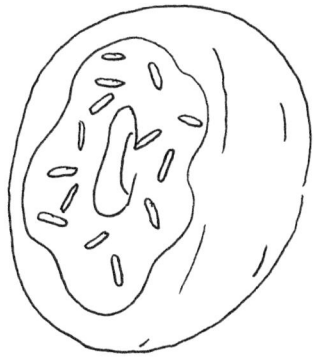

Because Grandma is not King John.

To explain the difference between windows and doors.

Because not everything
needs to be climbed.

Because every boy needs a mummy (or daddy).

For the sake of the person sitting across the table from him.

Because they don't always have an exit strategy.

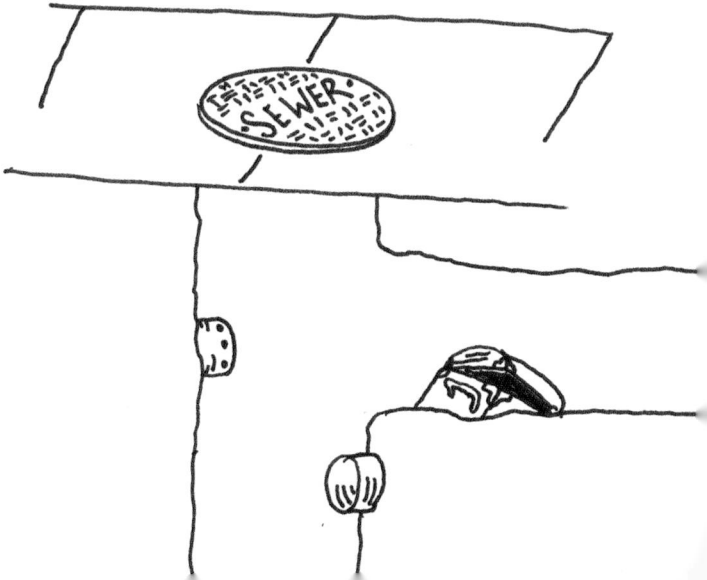

Because this happens.

Because an in-ground pool will not increase the property value.

Looking good.

To encourage their fashion sense.

Because they might be organic but they still don't go in the compost bin.

THIS WAS A STUPID IDEA
YEAH, LET'S TRY THE BLUE ONE
KEEP THIS GATE CLOSED

To foil their jailbreaks.

Because they share their snacks with the family member that licks its own butt.

Mom says it's good to share.

WE DEMAND LEMONADE.
AND COOKIES!

Because even the SWAT team needs backup.

Because he's not going to nag *himself.*

To conserve our natural resources.

To teach them where the food's supposed to go.

FOOD
HOLE
NOT
FOOD
HOLE

Because it might be hot, and he may be a dog, but you still cannot eat him.

To water them daily, so they'll grow.

Just one more!

To be their designated driver.

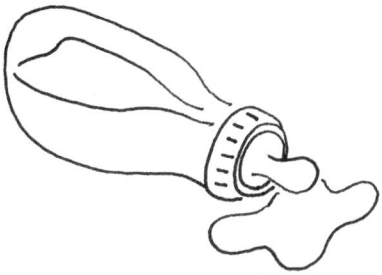

Because where there's smoke, there's a kid playing with illegal fireworks.

I've got to try this indoors.

SUMMER

Because sand feels better between your toes than up your nostrils.

To teach them the art of accessorizing.

Because they forget to cut out eyeholes.

ROBOT ALIENS
FROM
OUTER SPACE

Because they have the attention span of—oh look, a squirrel!

Because sometimes words fail.

Image Credits:

Cover: © GS/Gallery Stock
Page 04: © John Greim
Page 07: © Bernd Vogel/Corbis
Page 08: © Ocean Photography/Veer
Page 11: © Rubberball Photography/Veer
Page 13: © Design Pics/Super Stock
Page 14: © Pixaby
Page 17: © Super Stock
Page 18-19: © Super Stock
Page 21: © Age Fotostock/Super Stock
Page 23: © Stock Connection/Super Stock
Page 24: © Victoria Traig
Page 27: © Sarah Malarkey
Page 28: © Old Visuals/Classic Stock
Page 30: © Guido R. Rahr III
Page 33: © Cristina Miyar
Page 34: © Christina Rahr Lane
Page 37: © Stephen Mulcahey/Arcangel Images
Page 39: © Christina Rahr Lane
Page 40: © Nicole Hill/Rubber Ball
Page 42-43: © Mio Cade Photography
Page 44: © Tom Fernald
Page 46: © Leonard McCombe/Getty Images
Page 49: © Sean Murphy/Getty Images
Page 50-51: © Peter Mason/Getty Images
Page 52: © Jodie Griggs/Getty Images
Page 55: © Image Broker/Photo Shot
Page 57: © GS/Gallery Stock
Page 58: © Jay P. Morgan/Getty Images
Page 61: © Andreas Kuehn/Getty Images
Page 62: © Leana Alagia/Gallery Stock
Page 65: © Sean Murphy/Getty Images
Page 66: © John Lee/Blend Images

Page 69: © Cusp/Super Stock
Page 70: © Matt Edwards/Redcorn Studios
Page 73: © H. Armstrong Roberts/Classic Stock/Mary Evans Picture Library
Page 74: © Ariel Skelley
Page 77: © Radius/Corbis
Page 78: © Classic Stock/POUND/Mary Evans Picture Library
Page 81: © John Lund/Drew Kelly/Blend Images
Page 82: © Tony Watson/Arcangel Images
Page 85: © Tony Watson/Arcangel Images
Page 86: © Jenny Winkelman/David Liebman Stock
Page 88: © Allen Donikowski/Getty Images
Page 91: © Cameron/Corbis/AP Images
Page 92: © Jenny Winkelman/David Liebman Stock
Page 95: © Image Source/Super Stock
Page 96: © Lindsay Sablosky
Back Cover: © John Greim, © Rubberball Photography/Veer, © Jay P. Morgan/Getty